# MINNESOTA TIMBERWOLVES

## ALL-TIME GREATS

BY DAVID J. CLARKE

Book design by Jake Slavik
Cover design by Jake Slavik

Photographs ©: LM Otero/AP Images, cover (top), 1 (top); Andy King/AP Images, cover (bottom), 1 (bottom); Ken Levine/Allsport/Getty Images Sport/Getty Images, 4; Ann Heisenfelt/AP Images, 6; Peter A. Harris/AP Images, 8; Icon Sports Media/Icon Sportswire, 10; Kirby Lee/AP Images, 12; Jill Connelly/AP Images, 14; Mark J. Terrill/AP Images, 16; Brian Rothmuller/Icon Sportswire, 18; Abbie Parr/AP Images, 20

Press Box Books, an imprint of Press Room Editions.

**ISBN**
978-1-63494-664-3 (library bound)
978-1-63494-688-9 (paperback)
978-1-63494-735-0 (epub)
978-1-63494-712-1 (hosted ebook)

**Library of Congress Control Number: 2022919960**

Distributed by North Star Editions, Inc.
2297 Waters Drive
Mendota Heights, MN 55120
www.northstareditions.com

Printed in the United States of America
Mankato, MN
082023

# ABOUT THE AUTHOR

David J. Clarke is a freelance sportswriter. Originally from Helena, Montana, he now lives in Savannah, Georgia, with his golden retriever, Gus.

# TABLE OF CONTENTS

CAMPBELL
19

# CHAPTER 1
# YOUNG PUPS

The Minnesota Timberwolves entered the NBA in 1989. One of their first stars was guard **Tony Campbell**. In Minnesota's first season, Campbell led the team by averaging 23.2 points per game.

Campbell was joined by veteran forward **Sam Mitchell**. He had been playing professionally in France before signing with the Timberwolves in 1989. Mitchell was a steady player for 10 seasons in Minnesota.

LAETTNER
32

The Timberwolves struggled to win games early on. That meant the team had many high draft picks. In 1992, Minnesota used the third overall pick on **Christian Laettner**. The former Duke University forward had been one of the best college players ever. Minnesota fans hoped Laettner could be just as good in the NBA. Laettner became a good scorer. However, he never led Minnesota to the postseason.

The Timberwolves selected **Isaiah Rider** fifth overall in 1993. The flashy guard promised to win the dunk contest as a rookie. And he did. But Rider never became a superstar during the regular season.

GUGLIOTTA
24

In 1995, the team went through big changes. One addition was steady forward **Tom Gugliotta**. "Googs" played for seven teams in his career. He was at his best with Minnesota. Gugliotta eventually became an All-Star for the Timberwolves. Later that year, the team hired new general manager Kevin McHale to build a more exciting roster. Minnesota also got a new head coach that winter in Flip Saunders. But the biggest addition came at that summer's draft.

## FRIENDS FROM COLLEGE

Minnesota hired Kevin McHale as general manager in 1995. McHale had deep connections to the state. He grew up in Hibbing, Minnesota. He went on to star at the University of Minnesota in the 1970s. One of his teammates in college was Flip Saunders. McHale hired Saunders to be the Timberwolves head coach in December 1995.

GARNETT
21

# CHAPTER 2
# HOWLING

The Timberwolves had the fifth pick again at the 1995 draft. They used it on **Kevin Garnett**, a skinny forward from Chicago. Garnett was the first player to jump from high school to the NBA in nearly 20 years. And he soon became one of the league's most exciting players.

STAT SPOTLIGHT

## CAREER TRIPLE-DOUBLES
TIMBERWOLVES TEAM RECORD
**Kevin Garnett: 16**

SZCZERBIAK
10

Garnett was 6'11" and could play both outside and inside. He could score and rebound. But his defense was the best part of his game. Garnett's intense play made the team better almost right away.

A year after drafting Garnett, the Timberwolves added rookie point guard

**Stephon Marbury**. Sam Mitchell also returned after three years away. With those players and Tom Gugliotta, the Timberwolves finally made the playoffs in 1996–97.

That started a string of eight straight postseason appearances for Minnesota. But the Wolves were eliminated in the first round the first seven times. Players like Gugliotta and Marbury left the team during that time. They were replaced by players like smooth-shooting small forward **Wally Szczerbiak**.

The Timberwolves finally broke through in 2004. Garnett was now one of the league's top players. That year he won the Most Valuable Player (MVP) Award after averaging 24.2 points per game. He also led the NBA with 13.9 rebounds per game and the Timberwolves finally won a playoff series.

CASSELL
19

Two new players played a big role in 2003–04. The team's new point guard was veteran **Sam Cassell**. He was a tough defender and a good scorer. Cassell averaged 19.8 points that season. But he was also a smart passer who opened up scoring opportunities for others.

**Latrell Sprewell** was one of those scorers. The small forward chipped in more than 16 points per game. With three stars working together, the Timberwolves made the Western Conference finals. It was the best season in team history.

## HOMECOMING

Kevin Garnett left the Timberwolves in 2007. But he came back. Garnett spent the final 43 games of his career in Minnesota during the 2014–15 and 2015–16 seasons. In 2020, he became the first Minnesota Timberwolves player to enter the Basketball Hall of Fame.

LOVE
**42**

# CHAPTER 3
# THE NEW PACK

The Timberwolves dropped back down the standings after their playoff run in 2004. They added forward **Kevin Love** in 2008. He was another player who could pile up both points and rebounds. In one 2010 game, Love scored 30 points and grabbed 30 rebounds. No NBA player had done that in nearly 30 years. That year he made the first of three All-Star teams with Minnesota.

The Wolves didn't do much winning with Love on the roster, however. In 2014, he was traded to the Cleveland Cavaliers.

TOWNS 32

The Wolves got top draft pick **Andrew Wiggins** in return. The 6'6" swingman averaged more than 19 points per game over the next six seasons.

Minnesota selected **Karl-Anthony Towns** first overall a year after getting Wiggins. The 6'11" center had the strength to score inside. "KAT" was also a reliable three-point shooter. That made him one of the NBA's most dangerous scorers.

The pair helped lead the Wolves back to the playoffs in 2018. Wiggins was traded in 2020 for point guard **D'Angelo Russell**.

EDWARDS
1

The team's management thought the floor leader would be a better fit with Towns.

After a down season, the Timberwolves had the top pick again in 2020. Minnesota selected guard **Anthony Edwards**. "Ant" was an explosive athlete. That helped him average more than 20 points per game in his second season.

Edwards led the Timberwolves back to the playoffs in 2022 and 2023. The future looked bright in Minnesota.

## THE STIFLE TOWER

The Timberwolves made a big move after the 2021–22 season. They traded for center Rudy Gobert. The French big man had won the Defensive Player of the Year Award three times in his career. Minnesota fans hoped he would soon become another all-time great for the team.

# TIMELINE

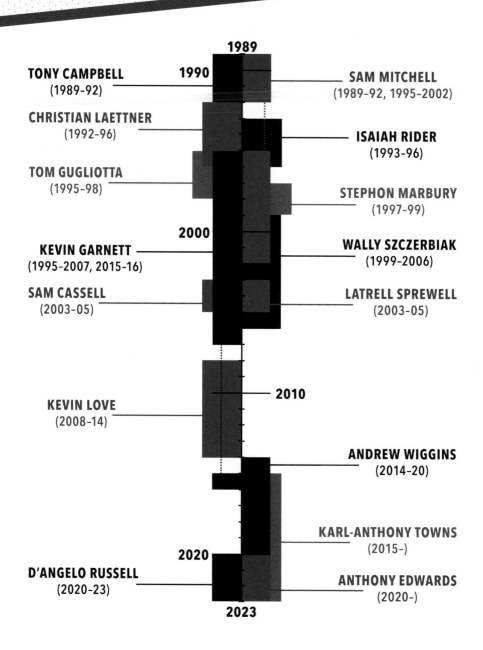

**1989**

**TONY CAMPBELL**
(1989-92)

**1990**

**SAM MITCHELL**
(1989-92, 1995-2002)

**CHRISTIAN LAETTNER**
(1992-96)

**ISAIAH RIDER**
(1993-96)

**TOM GUGLIOTTA**
(1995-98)

**STEPHON MARBURY**
(1997-99)

**2000**

**KEVIN GARNETT**
(1995-2007, 2015-16)

**WALLY SZCZERBIAK**
(1999-2006)

**SAM CASSELL**
(2003-05)

**LATRELL SPREWELL**
(2003-05)

**2010**

**KEVIN LOVE**
(2008-14)

**ANDREW WIGGINS**
(2014-20)

**KARL-ANTHONY TOWNS**
(2015-)

**2020**

**D'ANGELO RUSSELL**
(2020-23)

**ANTHONY EDWARDS**
(2020-)

**2023**

## MINNESOTA TIMBERWOLVES

**First season:** 1989–90

**NBA championships:** 0*

**Key coaches:**

**Chris Finch** (2021–)

62–61, 2–4 playoffs

**Flip Saunders** (1995–96 to 2004–05, 2014–15)

427–392, 17–30 playoffs

### MORE INFORMATION

To learn more about the Minnesota Timberwolves, go to **pressboxbooks.com/AllAccess**.

These links are routinely monitored and updated to provide the most current information available.

*Through 2021–22 season

# GLOSSARY

**conference**
A smaller group of teams that make up part of a sports league.

**draft**
An event that allows teams to choose new players coming into the league.

**general manager**
The person in a team's front office who drafts and signs new players.

**postseason**
A tournament for qualified teams after the regular season is over; another term for playoffs.

**rookie**
A first-year player.

**swingman**
A player who can play both guard and forward.

**triple-double**
When a player reaches 10 or more of three different statistics in one game.

**veteran**
A player who has spent several years in a league.

# INDEX